ABOUT FACE:

TURNING POINT TO DISCIPLINE

ABOUT FACE:

TURNING POINT TO DISCIPLINE

TASSHA FAISON

About Face: Turning Point to Discipline

Copyright © 2017 by Tassha Faison

All rights reserved. No part of this book may be repro-duced or transmitted in any form or by any means without written permission from the author.

ISBN: 978-0-9994648-4-7

Printed in the United States of America.

Book Cover Design: Yakeisha Biggs

FOREWORD

Discipline is a matter of the will. In order for us to achieve all that we are destined to accomplish, we must be faithful to the work. We all reach a place where a turning point is necessary. For many people, that time is now.

Tassha Faison encourages her readers to do a self-examination and face whatever decisions may be causing defeat in life. She understands that change is not immediate, but through reliance of God, His Word, and His instructions, life-altering transformation is inevitable.

Discipline does not have to be miserable, overwhelming, or disruptive. There can be joy in obedience when we keep our minds on the mission that God has given us. Developing positive daily practices will train us to desire to walk in a way that will bring rewards for consistency.

Allow Tassha to lead you through your personal turning point as you turn these pages. Face your fears, face your truth, and face your future. Embrace your discipline and step into your destiny!

Rekesha Pittman
Publishing Strategist
Get Write Publishing

TABLE OF CONTENTS

Chapter 1
The Turning Point – Discipline   1

Chapter 2
Maintaining Your Discipline   7

Chapter 3
Discipline and Your Loyalty   13

Chapter 4
Discipline and Your Duty   19

Chapter 5
Discipline and Your Respect   23

Chapter 6
Discipline and Your Selfless Service   29

Chapter 7
Discipline and Your Honors   35

Chapter 8
Discipline and Your Integrity   41

Chapter 9
Your Discipline and Personal Courage   47

Chapter 10
God and Your Discipline   53

About the Author

CHAPTER 1

THE TURNING POINT- DISCIPLINE

"For a man to conquer himself is the first and noblest of all victories."
-Plato

Awareness of the very importance of a proven and renowned venture would do no profiting without application of one's self to it. Going hard after the things which we believe in is a prerequisite to possessing our success from it. Jim Rohn points out that discipline is the bridge between goals and accomplishments. Merriam-Webster says goals are a set of things we want to achieve while accomplishments are successful completion of things set to do or things achieved. Goals are present or past while accomplishments are futuristic. Whether or not we get to the foreseen future is determined by our discipline.

Discipline is the practice of training people to obey rules, a code of behavior or using punishment to correct disobedience. It is crucial to establish that God emphasizes the importance and benefits of discipline. He also shows that He is ready to correct us when it seems as though we are walking astray.

"For whom the Lord loveth he chasteneth, and scourgeth every son whom he receiveth. If ye endure chastening, God dealeth with you as with sons; for what son is he whom the father chasteneth not?"
-Hebrews 12:6-7

"The hand of the diligent shall bear rule but the slothful shall be under tribute"
-Proverbs 12:24

He indicates to us a benefit attributed to discipline. Diligence is an off-shoot of discipline. The disciplined, principled individual is one to whom much is committed to because He is ready to walk aright for the actualization of the cause.

Let's look at the parable told by Jesus in Matthew 25:15-30 about the talents given to three different servants all belonging to the same master. Two of the three of them were diligent, disciplined, and understood the principle of sowing and reaping. They understood by discipline and practice, the dynamics of return on investments which they went ahead to practice when little was committed into their hands.

The Turning Point - Discipline

In verse 15 of that chapter, each of them had been commissioned with an assignment to bring about an accomplishment for their master.

"And unto one he gave five talents, to another two, and to another one; to every man according to his several ability; and straightway took his journey"
-Matthew 25:15

Each servant was given that measure of talent by their master because he gave them according to their capabilities and what they could reproduce when committed to an assignment. The first two were compelled to strive for double the amount of talents that were given. There was a reluctance and drawback in the third servant to accomplish anything meaningful and profitable with all that had been committed to him because he lacked the foresight to recognize that discipline bridges the gap between a goal (which was set for them by their master) and the expected accomplishment.

It is absurd and wrong for us to assume that all that has been committed into our hands by God will work themselves out without working and walking with God in full engagement for its fulfillment and not being involved.

Adam was an example of a man disciplined enough for God to trust him with the responsibility of tending the garden .

> ***"Faithful is he that calleth you,***
> ***who also will do it"***
> -1 Thessalonians 5:24

> ***"And the LORD God took the man,***
> ***and put him into the garden of Eden***
> ***to dress it and to keep it"***
> -Genesis 2:15

This was not an assignment for the slothful but for a man who had a vision. By discipline, he was able to lead and faithfully manage the garden. We must accept the fact that discipline is of the essence if we are going to transit through this terrestrial terrain successfully.

> ***"He that hath no rule over his own spirit***
> ***is like a city that is broken down,***
> ***and without walls."***
> -Proverbs 25:28

The success of any man on this earth is tied to his level of discipline. The many roles of the Holy Spirit in the life of a believer (which we will discuss at length in other chapters) include the chastening and correction as seen in 2 Timothy

3:16. God wants us to align our lives, decisions and accomplishments with Him. Through our discipline, the counsel of God comes to pass for us to full manifestation.

"We must suffer one of two things: the pain of discipline or the pain of regret and disappointment," as said by Jim Rohn. The degree to which we are ready to delay gratification for a brighter and greater future determines what we get out of life. Discipline is walking and acting as commanded, not as convenient. We must be able to put ourselves in order in all ramifications—spiritually, physically, emotionally, socially, financially, career-wise etc.

Avoiding or embracing discipline brings about the various consequences whether it be positive or negative.

CHAPTER 2

MAINTAINING YOUR DISCIPLINE

"It is not enough to have great qualities; we should also have the management of them."
-Le Rochefoucauld

Fire possesses a lot of benefits known to man but could cause a lot of harm when not controlled. Here in America, there have been told and untold stories of folks who got killed or harmed by fire. Wildfire destroys! So, also, discipline not maintained and curtailed could be the menace of society.

In October 2011, Terry Thompson and his wife, of the state of Ohio, had an alarming number of exotic pets. On that fateful day, he decided to release the animals, which included Bengal tigers, lions, wolves, and more into the neighborhood. After he did so, he killed himself. This posed a great threat to the environment as the man who had tamed these animals, whose voice and call they were used to, killed himself after releasing them. Sounds like a psychopath's mode of behavior, right? But this illustrates how many of us act in regards our discipline.

ABOUT FACE: TURNING POINT TO DISCIPLINE

Although our nation protects the rights of these animals and has bills passed for their safety and to help curb their extinction, the police had to kill nearly fifty of these animals as they could not be controlled and were dangerous.

This is a really horrific and tragic happening but it happened. The control and maintenance of our discipline brings about the safety of ourselves and others.

At one point or another, we have been in situations that have pushed us to the edge, almost trashing our prim and proper behavior. At times, due to the attitude of a waiter or the customer care personnel, for some of us, it was our direct boss who is in-charge of our long-awaited promotion but we had to maintain our discipline. Others have been blackmailed and by compellation pushed to compromise our standards as against our will, having the feel of total devastation afterward. This has been the case with many of us.

The largest room that exists is the room for improvement. Being ready to spend some time in this room to see the desired change is of great improtance. Going from where we are to the realm where we desire to be or see ourselves function is of utmost importance.

In Daniel 1:8, we see the non-compromise of Daniel, choosing to maintain his discipline despite the odds against him and his friends. This was a

Maintaining Your Discipline

big deal as this sometimes could bring about criticism. Most people are so concerned about what is being said about them that they begin to show a façade to those watching. They analyze their reputations until they forget who they truly are. It is easy to get lost trying to conform to the image of the world.

"But Daniel purposed in his heart that he would not defile himself with the portion of the king's meat, nor with the wine which he drank: therefore he requested of the prince of the eunuchs that he might not defile himself."
-Daniel 1:8

Conforming to the standards of the world is sending a signal for self-destruction. Maintaining discipline will steer destiny in the right direction for actualization.

William Feather and Horace respectively communicated about the essence for maintaining our discipline by saying, "If we don't discipline ourselves, the world will do it for us" and, "Rule your mind or it will rule you."

We see the essence of holding up our standards and maintaining our discipline in Daniel. He was a compendium of great capabilities, prin-cipled living, and the acknowledgment of the power of God in the lives of those ready to walk in his statutes. It is important to establish that God will never lower His standards for any of His creations at any point. That is why He showed that He is a constant and not a variable.

> *"And God said unto Moses,*
> *I AM THAT I AM: and he said,*
> *Thus shalt thou say unto the children of*
> *Israel, I AM hath sent me unto you."*
> -Exodus 3:14

Daniel was a man who took a stand in spite of opposition in most of his endeavors. He chose not to conform to the standards of the Babylonian kingdom and that made him indispensable. He earned a lifetime of relevance as a result of his stance. Maintaining his discipline created a rebound on those who wanted to tamper with his standards.

Our speech is a place of great vulnerability and where a great proportion of us need to learn to tame with urgency, as this is a tool of destruction and construction but this is greatly determined by the level to which we maintain our discipline in this area of great possibilities- whether they be positive or negative.

There are times when there is a need for silence—moments when silence is golden and we need to hold our peace in order to allow for progression and advancement. Sometimes we need to hold on to our view and let love rule.

Maintaining Your Discipline

**"What lies in our power to do,
lies in our power not to do."**
-Aristotle

This is not always the situation with many of us as we believe we ought to be fairly treated as others. It is very crucial to know that sometimes we've got to act the fool to fool the fools at times.

***"Wherefore, my beloved brethren,
let every man be swift to hear,
slow to speak, slow to*** **wrath:"**
-James 1:19

Christ understood the essence of maintaining his discipline in this speech and actions. Why take action? Why justify? Why speak for yourself? When at the end of it all, it will all turn to you for your uplifting. Instead, we say to ourselves, "I can't let him take advantage of me because he's my boss at the office. I would rather get a compulsory redundancy at the office than to be used."

Sometimes we've got to understand that God is working all things in our favor and would not leave us stranded at any point. He didn't bring us this far to abandon us to ourselves when we are committed to him. He remains committed to all who are committed to His cause.

ABOUT FACE: TURNING POINT TO DISCIPLINE

We have postulated the essence and need to maintain our discipline in all sectors of our individual lives which would reflect in all that we reach out to perform.

In the next seven chapters of this life-transforming book, we will be examining the seven core values of our nation's army- U.S. Army, their relation and correlation to the spiritual army rising as stated in the Bible for this end time.

"No man that warreth entangleth himself with the affairs of this life; that he may please him who hath chosen him to be a soldier."
-2 Timothy 2:4

CHAPTER 3

DISCIPLINE AND YOUR LOYALTY

"The test of true citizenship is loyalty to country."
-Bainbridge Colby

This quality in the officers of our army cannot be over-emphasized as this determines their patriotism to the nation.

The decision whether to sell America by causing a breach of security, or acting as a double agent for both America and those seeking for the fall of the nation, hangs in the balance of this essential quality to be expressed by all members of the Armed Forces.

In this 21st century, there have been allegations placed against individuals working for our agencies for selling classified information to other nations. Treason is an offense against a nation centered on disloyalty of which in some countries, the penalty for committing such crime is death. That's how vital the issue of loyalty is to a nation, but if it's that crucial, how come this quality lacks in a lot of individuals and becomes the menace of the society in this time and age?

In Revelations 22:10, John demonstrated his discipline by keeping to himself some of the prophecies given solely to him. He was able to retain the information to the end so that no other person possessed that particular revelation. This was a test of his discipline and loyalty to God.

One of the tests of being a prophet is not solely by a number of prophecies we are able to give and tell folks about the family tree but also the amount of information we can curtail from our various interactions with God and the realm of the spirit.

The only way a man's estate can be changed is by influencing his mind because he weighs information in this place of various weights pulling in different directions. His mind must be influenced in order for him to display the effect of his decision in his outward countenance because our attitudes, habits, and behaviors are guided by our current bag of knowledge. If we knew better, we would act better, live better, talk better and think better!

"If a man is not faithful to his own individuality, he cannot be loyal to anything."
-Claude McKay

Our loyalty and total allegiance to our nation, the U.S. Constitution, the U.S. Army, fellow soldiers and our prestigious nation's heritage all lie on our discipline and our loyalty to uphold them at all costs. It takes discipline to uphold our loyalty, even in the most absurd scenarios of life.

In Genesis 39, the story of Joseph is one that's well known. He was a slave in the house of Potiphar, handling all that went on in his house. Although a slave, Joseph remained faithful to the cause of prosperity of the house of Potiphar. All Potiphar was concerned with was entrusted to Joseph, including the food that he ate and even Potiphar's wife. His wife must have made advances toward Joseph before. The day that she framed him wasn't the first day he had experienced advances from her, but it was the day when he experienced the grand finale of her act.

In the middle of all her advances, Joseph remained loyal and gave his total allegiance to prosper the house of Potiphar in spite of the adversity he was facing. He made a commitment to not turn from his uprightness, even to his own detriment. Most men would rather eat the forbidden fruit than stand for that which they believe in and hold to be the truth.

A mind agreeable to compromise will choose not to delay gratification, which in turn damages them and places them in a position of reminiscing and regret. They might have wished they had not indulged in such acts and maintained loyalty at all costs. We ought to realize that we cannot eat our cake and have it, although, some of man's current inventions are gradually turning that saying obsolete.

As members of the end time army, we ought to submit to the dictates of this army which includes discipline and being loyal to its cause at all times.

First, we may evaluate ourselves and wonder how we are part of the spiritual army of the kingdom of God. The truth is that we are if we have come to understand that we are in the world and not of the world (1 John 2:16). We see illustrated here that walking with the Father exempts us from being part and parcel of the scourges of the world.

Evaluate yourself as an individual who has come to see that he has an assignment to deliver in this earth for the establishment of the kingdom of God here on earth (Isaiah 11:3). This is just to further establish to us that all that we are and have been created for a greater cause in the kingdom.

If we have accepted this as our reality, then we can head on to the next step; which is showing that all we have and will get involved in has a greater impact on more than just ourselves. It is also for the promotion of the kingdom of Him who has called us to be soldiers in His prominent dynasty.

Discipline and Your Loyalty

"For which I am an ambassador in bonds:
that therein I may speak boldly,
as I ought to speak."
-Ephesians 6:20

Paul is a patriarch of such high military ranking in the kingdom of God. He single-handedly wrote about two-thirds of the New Testament. In the above verse, he paid total allegiance to the kingdom of God by the use of the word "Ambassador."

According to the Merriam-Webster dictionary, an "ambassador," is a "diplomatic agent of the highest rank accredited to a foreign sovereign as the resident representative of his or her own government for a special and often temporary diplomatic assignment."

We know that we are high-ranking officials representing the noblest kingdom here in this terrestrial domain.

"Jesus answered them, Is it not written in
your law, I said, Ye are gods?"
-John 10:34

This hasn't dawned on many as we still live our lives carelessly and selfishly, thinking of just ourselves and family in all our daily pursuits. In this domain, we are here on a temporary assignment because the end of the world is very much at hand and we, as ambassadors, don't have all eternity to fulfill our assignments. We are constrained by time for we were fired down from the timeless zone (eternity) into a specified time zone (earth) to make this a working possibility to all who care to turn to the kingdom agenda paying utmost allegiance.

CHAPTER 4

DISCIPLINE AND YOUR DUTY

"In doing what we ought we deserve no praise because it is our duty."
-Joseph Addison

Carrying out what is expected of us should be seen as a norm through giving out to humanity and those around us. This hasn't been the case with us. We are selfish beings who seek to be praised for every stride we make in the direction of others to impact their lives. This ought to be the order of the day in our lives—living for others.

In Exodus from chapter 2 to chapter 40, we can see the birth, life, trials and the tribulations Moses experienced. We know that he was a man born and ordained for the deliverance of God's people from captivity and lasting about four centuries in the claws of the Egyptians. This was the place of assignment for Moses. His place of duty and obligation was in the deliverance of God's people which he had to carry out. He had

ABOUT FACE: TURNING POINT TO DISCIPLINE

to remain committed to take God's people to His ordained place for His people.

There were times when Moses could have quit due to the pressure and uproar from the people to which he had been chosen to lead. They were disobedient, nonchalant, and exhibiting several characteristics that could wear down any leader. Moses was the man with the largest congregation in the Bible but he kept his cool and handled the pressure, performing his duty and obligation to the people and to the One above who had called him to the place of leadership, influence, and affluence.

In an event of extreme provocation, he resorted to an open display of anger, which prevented him from entering into the Promised Land. Despite this, he remained committed and faithful to his assignment.

Mankind is known to carry out duties and obligations that will benefit themselves and their immediate families, as is known to think in a selfish manner.

Evaluate yourself. Imagine if you were a beneficiary of a particular inheritance of your wealthy father but had to share his wealth with the rest of your siblings. How would you feel? Would you partake in that? Moses, knowing that he wasn't going to taste the sweetness or see the glamour of the Promised Land, still led the children of Israel into Canaan-land. This was a challenge because he could see it from afar but not enter into the rest. Those who had been rebellious to God on several occasions still entered in, yet, Moses remained a man full of courage. He understood that he was working for the greater good of others and not just for himself.

How can this be? Why should God act so unjust and in an irrational manner? How could He do this to a man who had played a significant role in the deliverance of the people of God? He had risked his life and was on the verge of death at some point, from which he fled for his life to fulfill his duty and obligation. How could God have left him, to his own demise?

What we fail to realize is that as leader to whom much has been committed to by the hands of the Most High; to those of us to whom God has committed generations and assignments to; much is expected from us as God treats a leader with a higher level of chastening than he would treat a child in the faith who's learning to distinguish and discern between good and evil.

"But he that knew not, and did commit things worthy of stripes, shall be beaten with few stripes. For unto whomsoever much is given, of him shall be much required:
and to whom men have committed much, of him they will ask the more."
-Luke 12:48

ABOUT FACE: TURNING POINT TO DISCIPLINE

Men of the heavenly battalion show forth a high level of dedication, obligation, and duty for the promotion of the kingdom. Our responsibility here in this terrain ought to be followed with great discipline and obligation. We have been called into this great army and into the ministry of reconciliation, whereby we engraft and show others the way who also have been called.

There are a lot of soldiers who have been distracted from their line of duty and have been taken away with the cares of this world, they have been choked up with the affairs of this life and have taken their eyes off the mandate of the kingdom of God which has been committed into their hands.

Majority of the soldiers have had their minds gone with the wind and have lost their focus to one true cause to which we are to be committed to. We are men who have called to serve the greater cause despite the undoing and unfaithfulness of others outside the marching army which has been called to arise in this time and age to soldier on, expanding and exalting the kingdom of God in the various spheres of life and ministry.

"The superior man is the man who fulfills his duty."
-Eugene Ionesco

CHAPTER 5

DISCIPLINE AND YOUR RESPECT

"I fear God and respect God and love God."
-Brett Ratner

Our sense of value from our fellow individuals determines the flow of virtue from them to us—the kind of rreturn we get from them varies. The extent to which we revere God determines how much we receive from Him and what we can experience from Him.

> ***"...for them that honour me I will honour, and they that despise me shall be lightly esteemed."***
> -1 Samuel 2:30

The word "revere" doesn't show us as being weaklings wanting to please someone who is greater than us to have access to the favor to which they provide for us, but according to Merriam-Webster's dictionary, "revere" shows "one who is worthy of great honor."

We do not approach in beggarly manners when in their presence but regard them in high esteem. Our discipline and our respect go hand-in-gloves. They are not mutually exclusive to each other but they work as a complimentary version of themselves. Reverence to God or other mere men like ourselves grant us access to receiving from them.

> *"The fear of the Lord*
> *is the beginning of wisdom..."*
> -Proverbs 9:10

Every bonafide son and daughter of the kingdom of God who has chosen to take his or her place in this end-time army, as one on an assignment with great eternal value, is one who is disciplined and possesses the behavioral expression and pays cognizance to the need for respect in all endeavors for the source of a thing determines the DNA characteristics, abilities and tendencies of that thing.

> *"They shall run like mighty men;*
> *they shall climb the wall like men of war;*
> *and they shall march every one on his ways,*
> *and they shall not break their ranks:"*
> -Joel 2:7

We are military officers in the kingdom of God and as ones who have been engrafted into the kingdom of light from the kingdom of darkness. Individuals who have had their hearts and mind changed and turned towards the kingdom of God. We ought to walk and raise our heads up high as those who truly are or the higher order on this terrestrial ball. We operate as new creatures which we are by the finished work of Christ on the cross of Calvary.

God is principled and every one of His offsprings, which are we, ought to live principled lives. He showed His level of discipline and His commitment to retaining the respect of all that He created right from the commencement of the origination of man and other creatures here on earth.

He is a just God. He drove man out of the garden once he violated His voice which instructed him to do otherwise than he had done. This was because God had spoken and in order for Him to revere and keep His Word, man had to be driven out of the garden for not one jot of His Word would go unfulfilled without achieving what it was sent to do.

"So he drove out the man; and he placed at the east of the garden of Eden Cherubims, and a flaming sword which turned every way, to keep the way of the tree of life."
-Genesis 3:24

ABOUT FACE: TURNING POINT TO DISCIPLINE

The Golden rule is also known as the ethic of reciprocity which according to humanists believe that people should be treated in like manner, with compassion and consideration as they would love to be treated.

Adam did not walk in this manner, instead, he violated it. This is also the law which Jesus instituted during His time here on earth in Matthew 22:39 "...thou shall love thy neighbor as thyself." Adam violated this and he paid dearly for it at the expense of the lineage of mankind. No one would love to be treated in a manner where he is disregarded and his wisdom is not voiced. We don't want to be in places where we are tolerated as one of the burdens of life which folks must come across in the journey of life. Everyone wants and looks forward to being loved, respected, and revered by others, but how many individuals are willing to give such love, care, compassion, and consideration such as they received from others?

It's quite difficult to find such individuals who have allowed the love of God to overwhelm their hearts and who seek the good of others and have come to realize that a life lived for others is a life which is worthwhile, as said by Albert Einstein.

Joseph was an embodiment of the communion between discipline and respect. He had every opportunity to disregard any form of discipline seeing that he had experienced troubles and sorrows almost all through his life and could have given in to the contrary situations around him. He was the subject of envy amongst his father's children for the love and favoritism expressed toward him by his father at most times. This brought about great hatred from his elder siblings at that time. He was to be killed but sold off into slavery.

In a nation of slavery, Joseph always upheld his discipline and respect. He never gave in to compromise. Not once did he hang up his distinguishing qualities which he possessed for even one day. He remained faithful to himself. He exercised his respect for God, Potiphar, Potiphar's wife, and himself when he was tempted to sin in the absence of Potiphar, but in the presence of God. He upheld his worth by not crashing as most men of today would gladly dive into, not letting the opportunity go or forgetting that before breakthrough comes trials that could cause one to abort destiny. He refused, which landed him into greater trouble. He retained his worth and kept the faith, not relenting for one day to the end that whilst still in prison he was made the keeper and in charge of all that were in there with him.

As men and women who are functioning in accordance with the dictates of our General Commander who is up above, we ought to reflect on such portrayal of the true picture of whom we have been called to be and represent.

CHAPTER 6

DISCIPLINE AND YOUR SELFLESS SERVICE

"True greatness, true leadership, is achieved not by reducing men to one's service but in giving oneself in selfless service to them."
-Oswald J. Sanders

We ought to be able to see further for the greater good of others rather than just fending for ourselves and daily needs. This is against the regular notion which has infiltrated the society in which we live in today. Every man looks to cater for his daily troubles, needs, and wants. This ought not to be the case.

The conformation of the mind and the hearts of men to think in this direction in their quest for survival until they pass on is living a life of destitution, short-sightedness, and having a mind yet to be enlightened. We may be educated but not enlightened. There is a great difference in both realms. An educated man who isn't enlightened knows about a thing but it has no ripple effect on his mind and mode of thinking and actions. Enlightened individuals have been educated and have allowed the knowledge which they have gathered by education, permeate their being and they are walking in the light of all they have been able to gather by books and experientially. They are ready to give themselves wholly unto the dictates of what they have seen and what their hands have been able to handle.

The purity, taming, and enlightenment of the mind are of complementary association with the educated intellect. What shall it profit a man if he has been to three degrees of higher learning but manifests as one who has been on the countryside watching the bullock grow into maturity all his life? The application of self to selfless service is great gain.

The apostles in Acts 6:1-3 were front liners in Jesus' ministry. He committed the church into their hands to preach the good news, set the captives free and deliver them from the oppression of the enemy. In the above text, we see that the apostles consciously set some over the welfare of the widows and those in need at that time.

"And in those days, when the number of the disciples was multiplied, there arose a murmuring of the Grecians against the Hebrews, because their widows were neglected in the daily ministration. Then the twelve called the multitude of the disciples unto them, and said, It is not reason that we should leave the word of God, and serve

tables. Wherefore, brethren, look ye out among you seven men of honest report, full of the Holy Ghost and wisdom, whom we may appoint over this business."
-Acts 6:1-3

They were meticulous in their selection of those going to work attending to the welfare of the needy. They did not want any for embezzlemint as is rampant even in the church. They put up qualifications which depicted the willingness to serve, showing that they needed men of honest report who were down to earth and would serve humanity at every cost. They were willing to sacrifice their time, money, resources, energy, and intellect combined with their spiritual lives to service and ensure those who needed help received it at all costs.

Life isn't about what we can get and gain from it. It's primarily about what we can give back to life. If everyone who was born grew with the mindset that he or she ought to add value to the lives of others and give back to society, being of great impact and value adding, life would be a lot much better than it is today.

Queen Esther was enthroned after the display of pride which led to the banishing of Queen Vashti. Her enthronement was the deliverance of the Jews in process. She afflicted her body in fasting and was willing to sacrifice all she was (her

Queen) and all she would ever be (her future) for the greater good of those she represented in the palace (the Jews). She, just like Jesus, despised the shame which her death would have brought upon her and approached the throne of the King with the petition for the salvation of the people who she had been called to deliver.

Esther stood against all odds because she ought not to go into the King's chambers unless she was requested for which she did and obtained favor in the sight of the King. The Agagite had gone before the King aforetime and orchestrated evil for the Jews to lead to their total wipeout to be done in a day but were delivered by a selfless service of a woman who exalted the existence of the people she led above herself and gave herself to the demands of service.

She was willing to lay her life and her all for the deliverance of the people of the Jewish order.

"Go, gather together all the Jews that are present in Shushan, and fast ye for me, and neither eat nor drink three days, night or day: I also and my maidens will fast likewise; and so will I go in unto the king, which is not according to the law: and if I perish, I perish.

So Mordecai went his way, and did according to all that Esther had commanded him."
-Esther 4:16-17

Discipline and Your Selfless Service

More often than not, we get carried away by looking and making decisions just looking and thinking of ourselves but putting forth little or no consideration for those around us.

The creation of man in the image and likeness of God puts man in the position to always see beyond himself of which many have faltered. He is God and that puts all into consideration before making His move. We must act like folks from above, representing one who is greater than us and whose agenda we are ready to walk by at all times.

"Do some selfless service for people who are in need. Consider the whole picture, not just our little selves."
-Nina Hagen

CHAPTER 7

DISCIPLINE AND YOUR HONOR

**"Discipline is the soul of an army.
It makes small numbers formidable;
procures success to the weak
and esteem to all."**
-George Washington

The army and discipline are a similitude of each other. When we are told of the word army, the next terminology that we ought to think of is discipline. An army not disciplined is not an army, for their conquering ability is in their level of discipline which procures honor to all in the army.

Honor is of great value which cannot be purchased with the universal purchasing power of man in the financial world—money. It is bestowed on individuals for their level of good courage and accomplishment in their given endeavors. It is a product of giving back to humanity than what you received from it. It gives esteem to all from the accomplishment of a great feat and task.

The great Spanish soccer teams are seen as armies whose leaders are their coaches. Their coaches lead the team of colonels, lieutenants, captains etc. to the war front which is on the soccer pitch to battle against the opposing team in order to attain success for all. Those who end up on the bench as a result of injuries are still partakers of the success and esteem procured for all; for they are all on the same team and what applies to one because of the success of the battle is applicable to all within the team as long as they profess and plead their allegiance to the team and its leader.

David was a mighty man of war along-side his forty men of valor. They were men of great strength and skill and could singlehandedly take on multitudes of opposing armies. They were part of the army which David himself trained. He won many battles with the aid of these men.

One of David's mighty men could slay three hundred of the enemy's army. That was a strong man! We hardly know the names of all men in the army of David but one thing we know was that they were mighty men of valor trained by David and could not be conquered.

"These also are the chief of the mighty men whom David had, who strengthened themselves with him in his kingdom, and with all Israel, to make him king, according to the word of the LORD concerning Israel. And this is the number of the mighty men whom David had; Jashobeam, an Hachmonite, the chief of

the captains: he lifted up his spear against three hundred slain by him at one time."
-1 Chronicles 11:10-11

Having honor along with discipline is being prepared to fail with honor rather than succeed by fraudulent means. As said by Sophocles, you may have a great reputation with others, but within yourself, you are well-convinced that you are a man of a deformed character.

"A good name is better than precious ointment; and the day of death than the day of one's birth."
-Ecclesiastes 7:1

Reputation is without, while character is within. Reputation may be what other people, family, friends, colleagues, employers, and employees perceive. Character is who you really are and know on the inside that you truly are. Your character cannot be mistaken by you for any reason, but your reputation can be mistaken—even by others. Seeking the approval of everyone about your character is a sign of self-destruction, as you would move to please everyone to escape their criticism and gain their favor. Jesus said, woe unto you if all men speak well of you (Luke 6:26).

Our honor is not tied to the abundance of favorable speeches but lies in our character and level of discipline we have developed before. This brings about consequential honor in our dealings. In our functioning army, (the army of the kingdom of God), we understand that we ought to take responsibility for the kingdom. We must stop taking away from the kingdom and start adding to the kingdom in all spheres.

A man of honor engages in the lives of others who have lost their dignity and looking out for them and ensuring they live lives whose lost dignity has been restored or in the process of renewal and restoration.

> *"But if any provide not for his own,*
> *and specially for those of his own house,*
> *he hath denied the faith,*
> *and is worse than an infidel."*
> -1 Tim 5:8

It is a thing of great dishonor to any individual who cannot provide for his or her family, while possessing the capabilities to do so. Many have interpreted this verse of scripture to be referred only and exclusively to men but to societal beliefs that the man ought to be the sole provider for the family, which isn't true. He is the primary provider for the home, but not the sole provider. Such a person is seen to be without honor for honor is not purchased. We receive this as our reward for giving to society and to humanity out of the

Discipline and Your Honor

abundance of what we have and what's in our capacity to perform for the greater good of others.

We need to envision life, not just for our immediate relatives, but also for those who are without privilege.

Being decorated with the National Humanities Medal in the United States happens because of adding value, restoring the dignity, and providing to the human race what would not normally be done by any man. This is given in honor of exceptional gestures to mankind. As the famous Nobel prize won by authorities in different spheres of life is given for their tremendous achievements and the measure to which they have given to the society, rewards will come when we bring a change in the lives of many. It is given to acknowledge their heart which has been poured out to see others succeed in their life's work.

CHAPTER 8

DISCIPLINE AND YOUR INTEGRITY

"Power is actualized only when word and deed have not parted company."
-Hannah Arendt

The credibility of an ambassador is as crucial as the person or nation he represents for if he's a fraud, his nation would be seen as a fraud. They endorsed him representing them and can vouch for every form of behavior he exhibits at every point in time. Sending a man whose integrity is questionable as an extended personality of the Managing Director is a catastrophic scenario. Whatever he says is seen as directly from the Managing Director whether they be true or false. In the choice of an extended personality for a credible, high profiled societal individual, the extent of scrutiny to the integrity of the representative ought to be highly considered for any tarnish to the image of the representative causes a ripple effect on the represented.

Coming to terms that a man is equal to his words is of the essence. Don Miguel Ruiz shares his thought by saying, "Be impeccable with your

word. Speak with integrity. Say only what you mean. Avoid using the word to speak against yourself or to gossip about others. Use the power of your word in the direction of truth and love."
A man *is* his words, for his words are a product of his thought patterns and the things he has been meditating on.

Bringing a man from the slums of Queens to the White House wouldn't automatically change his perception of life in a day. An expectation for this in such a short time frame is a joke for you have to change the internal state of a man's mind before you change his estate. Why? Because his life and thought patterns have been channeled into a particular direction which informs his behavioral pattern and response to various issues of life.

Many individuals who profess the name of Christ have been found wanting in their integrity. They have not been able to show that that which they profess has become their profession. Scandals of ministers duping and running over members of their sheepfold are the order of the day on various media channels who would gladly promote such detrimental information. They have failed to uphold that which is good and given themselves to the condemnation of man, and ultimately, God if they fail to change their ways to live a life filled with integrity.

God and Your Discipline

This quality to be shown by men and women of the army of the Lord is almost equal to the quality of trust. Once the integrity of a man has been tarnished, it's an uphill task to reconstruct and return to the state of perfect integrity. Just like an egg, putting it together can never be the same anymore. It would have been shattered before we can put it together again.

Abraham was a friend of God's who had great integrity but he tampered with his integrity when he was face to face with a challenge in the presence of the King of Gerar. Abraham feared for his life and couldn't bear the thought in his heart if he lost his wife to King Abimelech, so he told a lie, referring to Sarah (his wife) as his sister. He knew that there was a tendency for him to be killed if he said she was his wife. He obtained mercy from and God appeared to the King in a dream of the night telling the King to return Abraham's wife to him or risk death. The king did not hesitate for he feared for his life and what God could do to him if he refused.

Abraham experienced mercy from God but the mercy of God which is available to us all should not be the basis and platform we take advantage of to lose our integrity.

"And Abraham said of Sarah his wife, She is my sister: and Abimelech king of Gerar sent, and took Sarah. But God came to

> ***Abimelech in a dream by night, and said to him, Behold, thou art but a dead man, for the woman which thou hast taken; for she is a man's wife."***
> -Genesis 20:2-3

There were men who were filled with this virtue—integrity—and have demonstrated the same in various aspects of their lives. Eventually this wasn't a loss to them in their endeavors.

Job was said to be a perfect and upright man. What a man, being referred to as a perfect man by God! That was quite some form of achievement. His integrity was acknowledged by God. He was not deceptive man, filled with cunning means of making a living. He was the richest man in the east at that time, but he was still referred to as a perfect and upright man.

> ***"There was a man in the land of Uz, whose name was Job; and that man was perfect and upright, and one that feared God, and eschewed evil."***
> -Job 1:1

Can we see this to be the case scenario with us in this time and age—being perfect and upright, despite our level of riches? Would we rather manipulate paying our taxes to the government in order to increase our net worth and be rated by

God and Your Discipline

Forbes, or we would rather pay our full taxes while upholding our integrity?

We don't have to cut corners in order to live the American dream. We don't have to cut corners to show how smart we are to our boss. We don't have to do wrong underground to show off to our fellow employees all because we want to escape the bitterness toward us. All these are vain and not profitable to us in anyway but lead to our undoing.

If you look toward the future, you would realize that with due diligence, consistency, and persistence, what others are cutting corners to achieve is going to work out favorably for you.

This has not been the case for many. We, especially of the younger generation, want to get everything done instantly—disregarding the principle of process. Why not wait to uphold your integrity? When you eventually get to the promised land, you won't be filled with shame and reproach for your acts of deceit in years earlier.

The process period is the time for gathering to know how to deal effectively with what has been prepared for you ahead.

"No man knows the importance of innocence and integrity but he who has lost them."
-William Godwin

CHAPTER 9

YOUR DISCIPLINE AND PERSONAL COURAGE

"To be courageous requires no exceptional qualifications, no magic formula, no special combination of time, place, and circumstance. It is an opportunity that sooner or later is presented to us all."
-John F. Kennedy

The display of courage is inevitable if we're going to stand out in our assignments which we have been given to perform and deliver as those handed the mandate of promoting the heavenly kingdom here on earth. Nothing can be done without the input and infusion of personal courage. Even if on a divine assignment, we must take our steps here on earth.

Facing the dreaded is inevitable. We must be aware that our peculiarity and similarity lies not only in our individual assignments but also in what we have to face in the accomplishment of them. Nothing can be achieved on our behalf if we cannot of ourselves step out of our comfort zones with strong will and determination.

ABOUT FACE: TURNING POINT TO DISCIPLINE

Time passing will bring us to vis-à-vis with situations where we must display our personal courage or we pay dearly for our inactions in such scenarios. It never alerts us before we encounter it but it is life's inevitable for men.

Joshua and Caleb were men who displayed such strong personal courage. They, alongside ten other spies, were sent to take a peek of the Promise Land to inform the takeover perpetuators on the kind of strategy, form of war, and weapons to prepare for the displacement of the possessors of the land. This required great courage, for those dwelling in the land were men of great stature and due to the lack of courage, ten out of twelve that were sent to spy on the Promise Land, saw themselves as grasshoppers at the face of the opposition. The exceptions were Joshua and Caleb with their loins girded up with personal courage to see those in the Promise Land as conquerable.

The ten spies tried to instill their lack of personal courage into the people of Israel so that they also would be without personal courage. Instead, Joshua and Caleb stilled the people. The people were already being convinced that they had no chance against the enemies and were already creating the image of lack of courage and defeat in their thoughts for they had been told that they were grasshoppers in the sight of the opposition.

God and Your Discipline

"Nevertheless the people be strong that dwell in the land, and the cities are walled, and very great: and moreover we saw the children of Anak there. The Amalekites dwell in the land of the south: and the Hittites, and the Jebusites, and the Amorites, dwell in the mountains: and the Canaanites dwell by the sea, and by the coast of Jordan. And Caleb stilled the people before Moses, and said, Let us go up at once, and possess it; for we are well able to overcome it. But the men that went up with him said, We be not able to go up against the people; for they are stronger than we. And they brought up an evil report of the land which they had searched unto the children of Israel, saying, the land, through which we have gone to search it, is a land that eateth up the inhabitants thereof; and all the people that we saw in it are men of a great stature."
-Numbers 13:28-32

Courage to conquer is directly linked with the kind of images we allow into our heart and mind. If we solely create images of defeat, depression, failure, and thoughts which feed on the fears of man, we can never rise with personal courage to take on the challenges that face us on a daily basis, for as a man thinketh in his heart, so is he (Proverbs 23:7).

ABOUT FACE: TURNING POINT TO DISCIPLINE

Whether we succeed or fail, it all started with images in our minds.

The display of personal courage or cowardice all starts in our minds and hearts. This is where our progress or retrogression commences from. Our enemy knows this and strikes from there. Once he can succeed in planting the wrong images and getting us to believe them as our reality, then he has won the battle pending when we realize this and are willing to change these images to ones of victory and advancement.

As regenerated sons and daughter of God, we should understand that we are fruitful vines but this can only happen when we look to conditioning our minds and hearts to what has been spoken of in the Word of God which is and forever shall be.

Courage doesn't mean you did not come in contact with the dreaded but it implies that you choose to stand your ground regardless of what may come your way or what you may see happen at any point. The two men, Joshua and Caleb, saw differently from others and they chose to stand by the kind of images which they had allowed to permeate their minds. They recognized that it requires no form of energy to stand in the crowd but great personal courage is needed for an individual to stand alone which they were willing to go all out for at what very extent to which it might cost them.

God and Your Discipline

"Fear is a reaction, courage is a decision"
-Winston S. Churchill

CHAPTER 10

GOD AND YOUR DISCIPLINE

This is ultimate!

We have been able to evaluate the need to maintain our discipline. We have also been able to correlate the relationship between the seven U.S. Army core values—which guide their every operation and is known as the modus operandi of every one of their recruits to the topmost ranking officer. We have been able to distinguish the essence of our loyalty and give all to the one to whom we pay our allegiance to.

The total and never relenting need to always pay the price and perform our obligation and duty at whatever cost and extent for which we have been cut out for such under any kind of pressure.

The same boiling water that softens potatoes hardens the egg. This is a result of the kind of stuff we are made of. The origination of a matter particle determines the level of pressure and what it can deal with each time. Respect is not demanded but earned. Respect is expressed in reciprocity. Being ready to give our all to others, living for the greater good of all and believing our lives are more than our immediate families depicts our readiness to live for humanity, performing and contributing our own quota of selfless service to our environment and all we converse with.

In our quest to live while serving others, we cannot chase our own the glory. We must perform all that we ought to efficiently, without honor being our motive. It must be a consequence of selfless acts towards others. Maintaining integrity in the pursuit of life and its goodness through the dispensation of our duties and obligation is crucial.

The manifestation of personal courage in all is inevitable as this determines whether or not we show the other characteristics mentioned above. We would be hampered by our inability to display this for without it we can do almost nothing.

> **"We need to understand the difference between discipline and punishment. Punishment is what you do to someone; discipline is what you do for someone"**
> -Zig Ziglar

Here in this concluding chapter, we would sojourn into the aspect of God and his mind on discipline. What He thinks about discipline, His motive for discipline, his mode of discipline, and what He aims at achieving from the act of discipline towards those He cherishes and loves.

The necessity of discipline cannot be over-emphasized enough. The more mature we are, the tougher our discipline is as it relates to God. Jesus shows us that those who have received much from above, much more is expected from such a person.

There is a difference in the expectation and the method of discipline between a 3-year-old child and a 15-year-old child. This is because the 15-year-old has more understanding than the 3-year-old. He has grown to understand some things that the younger wouldn't understand. This also applies with God; the higher our rank in His army, the more intense His discipline for us becomes.

Paul said when he was a child, he acted, spoke and his understanding was as a little child but when he grew into being a man he had to put away childish things and man up. That is, his acts, speech, and understanding had to be changed and conformed into that of a grown man, for he was no longer a child (1 Corinthians 13:11).

We should understand that those who experience the discipline of God are those whom He loves.

"And ye have forgotten the exhortation which speaketh unto you as unto children, My son, despise not thou the chastening of the Lord, nor faint when thou art rebuked of him: For whom the Lord loveth he chasteneth, and scourgeth every son whom he receiveth. If ye endure chastening, God dealeth with you as

with sons; for what son is he whom the father chasteneth not? But if ye be without chastisement, whereof all are partakers, then are ye bastards, and not sons."
-Hebrews 12:5-8

God never chastises those who are not his own. For you to be disciplined by God is a privilege for it further validates your sonship in the family and army of God. We can't be braggadocios about our authenticity in the family of God if we don't partake and take share in His chastening. His chastening worketh a greater good in us. If we be gold, we must pass through the fire!

Though it is painful, it is of great value to us in all ramifications.

"Now no chastening for the present seemeth to be joyous, but grievous: nevertheless afterward it yieldeth the peaceable fruit of righteousness unto them which are exercised thereby."
-Hebrews 12:11

We never want to experience this as it is never convenient and neither is it pleasant for us but we must go through it if we want to come out properly furnished, fit for the commander's use.

God and Your Discipline

It is known that the receiver of the discipline never sees the profitability of the discipline as much as the dispenser of the discipline for it is never a joyful passage.

We are never disciplined by God for the fun of it but we are disciplined for our own good. Discipline is a fire we will all pass through. As people, we will err at one point or another. We need to be put back on track at times.

Many times, we have no clue about what is going on regarding God disciplining us, but we must hold on in faith. Believe and know that He has good plans for us always, to bring us to an expected end which we have always hoped and longed for (Jeremiah 29:11).

For us to develop as well-trained men and women of the kingdom of God, we must be very disciplined and pay attention to the chastening of our heavenly Father. To opt out of God's discipline is of great danger, for that which fails to discipline you is not profitable to you.

Pastor Tassha Faison
Turning Point Life Coaching, LLC

Pastor Tassha Faison is the founder and CEO of United and Spiritually Armed Forces, Inc (2012) and Turning Point LLC, which was established in 2016 to help individuals, groups and entrepreneurs attain their goals.

She is also the Regional Director of Women with A Call International (WWACI) and President of a local WWACI Branch in Fort Hood, Texas under the Leadership of its Founder, Dr. Elizabeth Hairston-McBurrows. Tassha received several leadership awards while serving in the army. Though retired, Tassha remains a great asset to the soldiers who are still serving.

She has a heart for the Kingdom of God and her local community. Despite several turning points in her life, she has embraced the mandate always to impact lives in a positive manner.

ABOUT FACE: TURNING POINT TO DISCIPLINE

Her passion is helping others shape their lives physically, mentally and mostly spiritually because she comprehends that listening to God is essential for a successful life's journey.

A great motivator and purpose-driven minister of the gospel, Pastor Faison believes in empowering the whole man and not focusing on weakness.

Tassha earned a Bachelor of Science in Human Services. She later went on to obtain a Masters of Divinity with an emphasis in chaplaincy services. Tassha is also a graduate of The Apostolic/Prophetic Connection's, Inc (TAPC) under the leadership of Apostle Elizabeth Hairston-McBurrows.

Pastor Faison is the mother of two sons who are progressively pursuing their education and functioning as outstanding athletes in the community. She serves as administrative assistant for Apostle Elizabeth Hairston-McBurrows. She is also an entrepreneur, Author, mentor and a certified life coach with the John Maxwell Team.

www.ingramcontent.com/pod-product-compliance
Lightning Source LLC
Chambersburg PA
CBHW071414040426
42444CB00009B/2249